MOVIE FAVORITES

Solos and String Orchestra Arrangements
Correlated with Essential Elements String Method

Arranged by
ELLIOT DEL BORGO

Welcome to Essential Elements Movie Favorites! There are two versions of each selection in this versatile book. The SOLO version appears in the beginning of your book. The STRING ORCHESTRA arrangements of each song follows. The supplemental CD recording or string orchestra PIANO PART may be used as an accompaniment for solo performance. Use these recordings when playing solos for friends and family.

ISBN 978-0-7935-8421-5

HAL•LEONARD®
CORPORATION

7777 W. BLUEMOUND RD. P.O. BOX 13819 MILWAUKEE, WI 53213

0868022
nd Edition

From CHARIOTS OF FIRE

CHARIOTS OF FIRE

CELLO
Solo

Music by VANGELIS
Arranged by ELLIOT DEL BORGO

00868022

From the Paramount Motion Picture FORREST GUMP

FORREST GUMP-MAIN TITLE

(Feather Theme)

Music by ALAN SILVESTRI
Arranged by ELLIOT DEL BORGO

68022

4

APOLLO 13

(End Credits)

By JAMES HORN[...]
Arranged by ELLIOT DEL BOR[...]

CELLO
Solo

00868022

From DANCES WITH WOLVES
THE JOHN DUNBAR THEME

By JOHN BARRY
Arranged by ELLIOT DEL BORGO

CELLO
Solo

Expressively

B68022

From the Universal Picture E.T. (THE EXTRA-TERRESTRIAL)

THEME FROM E.T.
(The Extra-Terrestrial)

CELLO
Solo

Music by JOHN WILLIAM
Arranged by ELLIOT DEL BORO

MCA MUSIC PUBLISHING

00868022

THEME FROM "JURASSIC PARK"

Composed by JOHN WILLIAMS
Arranged by ELLIOT DEL BORGO

MCA MUSIC PUBLISHING

8

From THE MAN FROM SNOWY RIVER

THE MAN FROM SNOWY RIVER
(Main Title Theme)

CELLO
Solo

By BRUCE ROWLAN
Arranged by ELLIOT DEL BORG

MISSION: IMPOSSIBLE THEME

By LALO SCHIFRIN
Arranged by ELLIOT DEL BORGO

CELLO
Solo

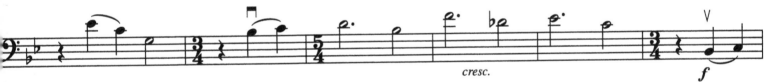

From the Paramount Motion Picture RAIDERS OF THE LOST ARK

RAIDERS MARCH

CELLO
Solo

Music by JOHN WILLIAM
Arranged by ELLIOT DEL BORG

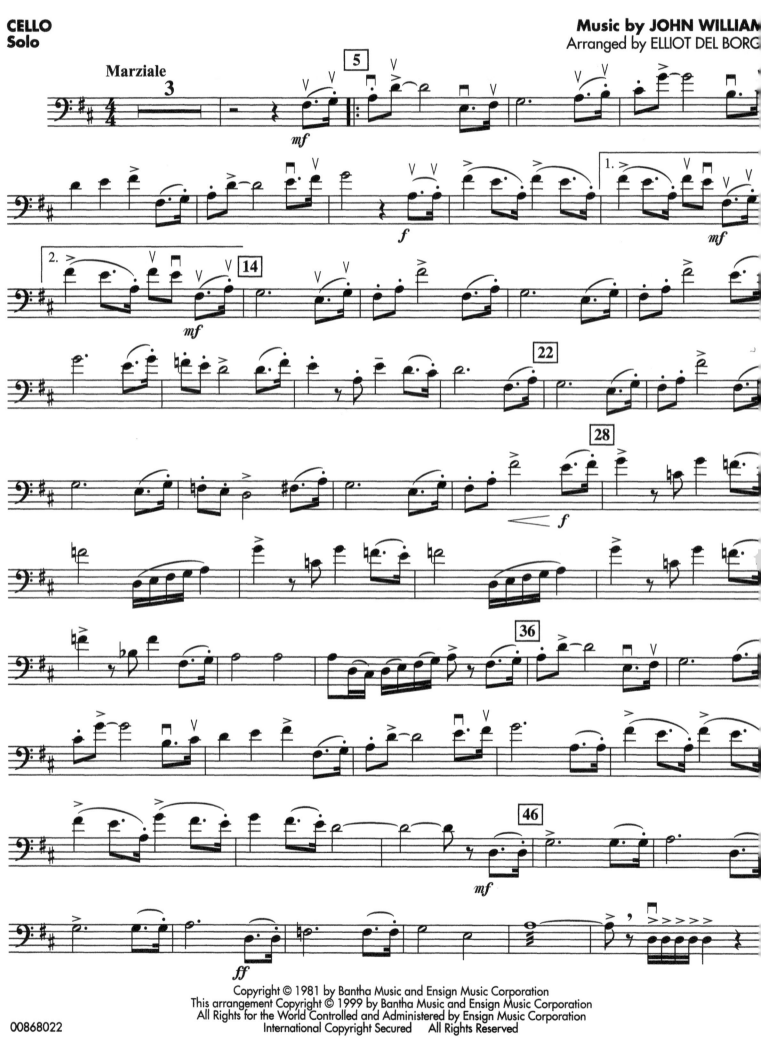

From AN AMERICAN TAIL

SOMEWHERE OUT THERE

Words and Music by JAMES HORNER,
BARRY MANN and CYNTHIA WEIL
Arranged by ELLIOT DEL BORGO

CELLO
Solo

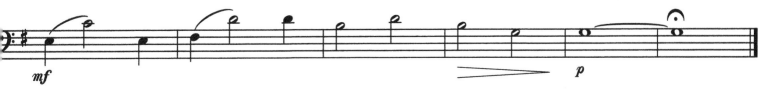

MCA MUSIC PUBLISHING

STAR TREK® THE MOTION PICTURE

CELLO
Solo

Music by JERRY GOLDSMITH
Arranged by ELLIOT DEL BORG

From CHARIOTS OF FIRE
CHARIOTS OF FIRE

CELLO
String Orchestra Arrangement

Music by VANGELIS
Arranged by ELLIOT DEL BORGO

Moderato

B68022

FORREST GUMP-MAIN TITLE

(Feather Theme)

CELLO
String Orchestra Arrangement

Music by ALAN SILVESTRI
Arranged by ELLIOT DEL BORGO

00868022

APOLLO 13

(End Credits)

By JAMES HORNER
Arranged by ELLIOT DEL BORGO

ELLO
tring Orchestra Arrangement

From **DANCES WITH WOLVES**
THE JOHN DUNBAR THEME

CELLO
String Orchestra Arrangement

By JOHN BARRY
Arranged by ELLIOT DEL BORGO

00868022

THEME FROM E.T.
(The Extra-Terrestrial)

Music by JOHN WILLIAMS
Arranged by ELLIOT DEL BORGO

CELLO
String Orchestra Arrangement

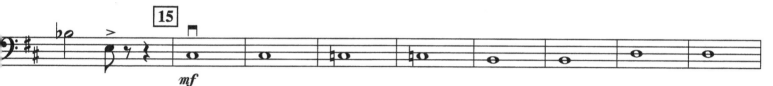

868022

MCA MUSIC PUBLISHING

From the Universal Motion Picture JURASSIC PARK

THEME FROM "JURASSIC PARK"

CELLO
String Orchestra Arrangement

Composed by JOHN WILLIAM
Arranged by ELLIOT DEL BORG

00868022

THE MAN FROM SNOWY RIVER
(Main Title Theme)

By BRUCE ROWLAND
Arranged by ELLIOT DEL BORGO

CELLO
String Orchestra Arrangement

0868022

From the Paramount Motion Picture MISSION: IMPOSSIBLE

MISSION: IMPOSSIBLE THEME

CELLO
String Orchestra Arrangement

By LALO SCHIFRIN
Arranged by ELLIOT DEL BORGO

RAIDERS MARCH

CELLO
String Orchestra Arrangement

Music by JOHN WILLIAMS
Arranged by ELLIOT DEL BORGO

0868022

From AN AMERICAN TAIL
SOMEWHERE OUT THERE

CELLO
String Orchestra Arrangement

Words and Music by JAMES HORNER
BARRY MANN and CYNTHIA WEIL
Arranged by ELLIOT DEL BORGO

00868022

MCA MUSIC PUBLISHING

STAR TREK® THE MOTION PICTURE

CELLO
String Orchestra Arrangement

Music by JERRY GOLDSMITH
Arranged by ELLIOT DEL BORGO